FANTASTIC FOOTBALL

Robin Bennett

Robin is an author and entrepreneur who has written several books for children.

Aged 21, he was all set to become a cavalry officer (in charge of tanks), and aged 21 and a half, he found himself working as an assistant grave digger in south London wondering where it had all gone wrong.

Robin Bennett plays most sports. Poorly.

Matt Cherry

Matt grew up on the Kent coast, writing and drawing, where he still lives today with his wife and two children. He still loves to write and draw every day, so he hasn't changed much really. He's just a lot taller.

STUPENDOUS SPORTS

FANTASTIC FOOTBALL

ROBIN BENNETT
ILLUSTRATED BY
MATT CHERRY

Firefly

First published in 2022
by Firefly Press
25 Gabalfa Road, Llandaff North,
Cardiff, CF14 2JJ
www.fireflypress.co.uk

A CIP catalogue record of this book
is available from the British Library.

1 3 5 7 9 8 6 4 2

ISBN 978-1-913102-91-3

*This book has been published with the support
of the Books Council of Wales.*

Design by: Becka Moor
Printed and bound by: CPI Group (UK) Ltd,
Croydon, Surrey CRO 4YY

CONTENTS

THIS BOOK BELONGS TO

CHAPTER 1:
THE HISTORY OF SOCCER

Football is one of those games that feels like it's been around **forever**.

For example, I think we can safely say that there were a lot of rocks just lying about the place during the Stone Age, hence the name: **The Stone Age**. Owing to the fact that quite a few of them were almost certainly:

⚽ a) roundish

⚽ b) getting in the way

⚽ c) small enough to hoof at your little brother,

it's very possible that football was first tried out by bored velociraptors or sporty mastadons.

Having said that, it was first played by actual **Human Beings** in China in a nice civilised way more than 2000 years ago as a game called Cuju. Then it went to ancient Greece and Rome before popping up in England calling itself '**foteballe**'. By which time it was *not* civilised; matches lasted days, involved hundreds of players, goals nearly three miles apart and so much fighting that it was banned by Edward II in 1314.

However, as a king, people rarely ever listened to Edward and they weren't about to start now, so football continued to be played in a rough and very violent way until the sixteenth century. It was at this moment in **Stupendous Sports** history that a schoolboy called Richard Mulcaster began to write excited letters home about playing a game with what Eton headteacher William Horman described at the time as 'a ball full of wynde' (pumped up, nothing to do with farts), that had set positions, a referee, coach and rules:

'*not ... shouldring one an other so barbarously ...*
by the chiefe use of the legges'
meaning: play with your feet, try not to kill your classmates.

This was all, presumably, instead of Master Mulcaster of Eton getting on with his Greek homework, which would definitely have made King

Edward (had he still been alive) very angry indeed. Fast forward a couple of hundred years and it was a combination of British schoolboys and the invention of trains that made the modern game what it is today.

⚽ Schoolboys, because they will do almost anything to avoid doing any actual work – so making up games is always going to be popular.

⚽ And trains, because you need something faster than the school donkey to get you to matches in places with other kids.

Cambridge Rules and Sheffield Rules were

the first form of competitive soccer developed so
people from different clubs and schools could be
a hundred per cent sure they had all turned up to
play the same game.

However, it's important at this point in our story
to say that football isn't just amazing because it's
really old **but** also because if it wasn't for football,
most other team games involving balls wouldn't
exist at all! This includes (in no particular order):
rugby, Gaelic football, Australian rules football,
American football (yup), underwater football,
something called **jorkyball** (if you only have three
friends) ... and babyfoot, which everybody agrees is
brilliant, so it is a sport as far as we at Stupendous
Sports are concerned.

COOL QUOTES

**'Winning doesn't really matter as
long as you win.'**
– Vinny Jones (member of Wimbledon FC's infamous
'Crazy Gang' during the 1990s and holder of the fastest
ever yellow card record at three seconds into a match)

Nowadays football is easily the most popular
sport in the world. According to **FIFA**, there are

over 250 million players playing in 200 countries with over 3.5 billion fans – nearly half the people in the world, whatever their gender, and even next-door's dog – with players of every age and ability!

As the biggest sport on planet Earth, it is very powerful. How players behave and the things they say, on and off the pitch, are listened to by millions. Football players are often more famous than presidents and pop stars. And getting richer by the minute.

In fact, the average premier league footballer's salary climbed from £45 a week in 1961 to £60,000 a week in 2020. And the highest paid players are on nearer £400,000 a week, which is enough money to  buy a Ferrari every couple of days and still have change left over for takeaways and sweets and the odd house.

Some people think this is a good thing – mainly the very rich and famous football players themselves (and their mums) – other people think it's a very bad thing. The rest of us just think it's a thing and get on with playing the game with our mates and having fun watching it on the telly.

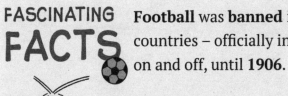

FASCINATING FACTS

Football was **banned** in a lot of countries – officially in Scotland, on and off, until **1906**.

Football, association football and **soccer** are different names for the same thing.

Women have been playing association football almost **as long as men**. However, during the First World War, women's football was possibly **bigger** than the men's game. And on Boxing day 1920, Dick, Kerr Ladies against St Helens Ladies was watched by a gigantic **53,000** people at Goodison Park, with more than **14,000** more spectators locked outside the stadium. The ladies were **proper celebrities**. And none more so than **Lily Parr**. Almost six feet tall with one of the most powerful kicks in the game – she even **broke a goalie's wrist** once, when they tried to stop her shot at goal.

A FUNNY THING HAPPENED

There is evidence that football was played in many parts of the world. In **1586** an English explorer called **John Davis** came across a tribe of Inuits from Greenland playing the game, stopped his ship and joined in.

Great dates

1174 (roughly) First mention (by William FitzStephen) of modern football.

1526 The royal footwear collection recorded that Henry VIII owned one of the first pairs of football boots.

1824 World's first football club formed in Edinburgh.

1857 One of the oldest professional football clubs, Sheffield FC, formed. Several other clubs also claim to be the first professional football clubs, including Notts Country, Cambridge and Crystal Palace.

1871/2 The Football Association Challenge Cup (FA Cup) became the first important competition. The final was played at the Oval cricket ground.

1872 First International between Scotland and England: 4000 spectators watched a no-score draw.

1891 Penalty kick first introduced: Germany deliriously happy.

1894 The British Ladies' Football Club formed. First match watched by over 11,000 spectators.

1904 FIFA founded by France, Belgium, Denmark, Netherlands, Spain, Sweden and Switzerland.

1908 Football first played competitively in the Olympic Games.

1930 First Men's Football World Cup in Uruguay, won by Uruguay (4-2 against Argentina).

1991 First Women's World Cup in China.

MESSI

Captained Argentina, most capped player for his country, winner of seven BALLON D'OR, scorer of over 750 professional goals, FIFA Men's player of the year ... all round smartypants basically.

I was lucky to see Messi play once in Barcelona. It was a match against REAL MADRID and I was in the perfect position to see Messi score a goal – except from where I was sitting (I was right behind him) he didn't stand a chance – it was an impossible shot. There was literally no way through two defenders and the goalkeeper. But I was wrong: Messi did something with his feet, his hips, his hands ... it was like a magic trick which fooled me and the defenders, before slotting the ball casually into the back of the net. I've never seen anything like it. If that had been me, I would have done a breakdance, followed by cartwheels and somersaults for the next five minutes and phoned my mum, but Messi just gave a slight smile and waved at the fans. All in a day's work.

Messi is not the strongest defender, or the
fastest attacker, or the best jumper (he's a
bit short, to be fair). But he's arguably the best
player in the world today and definitely one of the
best to have ever played the game.

WHY?

Well, there's his dribbling ability.
Not the fastest runner without the ball, but there
are very few players who are better at dribbling,
especially with his 'magic' left foot. He keeps
the ball close and moves like lightning ... but most
incredibly he makes it look EASY.

PATIENCE

Because of his reputation, other players will stop him
getting into the game by swarming about Messi like
angry bees as soon as he gets anywhere near the ball.
Messi will often seem out of a game for most of it
... then, just when no one is expecting it, he'll strike.

INTELLIGENCE

Like all the best players, he can see what is
happening in a game without looking and sometimes
before it happens. Being able to tell where to put a
pass or run into space before anyone else is a big
advantage.

ACCURACY

One of the reasons he's scored so many goals is
not how hard he kicks the ball but how it is nearly
always ON TARGET. Unlike most of us, you very
rarely see him hoof it half a mile over the goal or
so wide of the posts it hits a cameraman in the
face.

He is a lot of people's favourite player, including
David Beckham.

CHAPTER 2: MEET THE PLAYERS

Positions in football aren't as fixed as in some sports, like rugby or American football (which shouldn't really be called football, because it's mainly played with your hands). This means that not all the positions in football are used every time you play, which also gives teams more choice when they decide to have attacking or defending formations ... or 'hang about sort of in the middle' formations.

Not having fixed positions is one of the reasons football is so fast moving and exciting.

That said, every team needs a **goalkeeper** and then a few **defenders** to make sure the goalie isn't left all on their own for ninety minutes, then you need **forward** players or goals don't get scored, and that leaves a large empty green bit in between everyone that you need to fill up, so we have **midfielders**.

There are usually eleven players on each team (including the goalkeeper), and apart from utility players – clever clogs who can play anywhere on the pitch – most players are quite specialist.

STUPENDOUS SPORTS TRUMPS (based – more or less – on 4-4-2 system, see page 65)

1. GOALKEEPER

⚽ Comedy big hands: **10**
⚽ Catching: **10**
⚽ Leaping sideways: **10**
⚽ Bravery: **10**
⚽ Pain threshold: **10**
⚽ Boredom threshold: **8**
⚽ Tasteful kit: **3**

A good **goalkeeper** needs to be as agile as a cat that's just found itself a cramped cupboard full of poisonous spiders, whilst also being very tall and with hands you can easily see from space. It also helps if you don't mind being kicked in the face by muddy boots, hit in the face by soggy balls, or having strikers on the other team shout in your face. You'll also spend most of the game jumping about on the spot like you're trying to look over a garden fence ... but this just to stay warm.

Truth is, unless you don't like running, it's a

tough position to play. But save a penalty kick and you'll shine brighter than the sun.

DEFENDERS

2. RIGHT BACK AND 3. LEFT BACK

⚽ Ability to charge about for ninety minutes without stopping: 10
⚽ Tackling: 10
⚽ Shins like iron bars: 10
⚽ Tactical ability of a tenth-century Mongol general: 10
⚽ Heading the ball: 10
⚽ Friends with strikers: 8
⚽ Having nightmares about scoring own goals: 1

Sometimes called a **Full Back**, you need to be very good at running backwards, forwards and sideways – often all at the same time. Positioned closest to the touchline, at the back, your role is defensive when the ball is with the other team and attacking when your side has possession.

If a team is playing more **Centre Backs** (see next card), then the position is sometimes turned into a **Wing Back** and made more of an attacking position.

So, apart from running about a lot, good **Full Backs** need to have an excellent idea what is going on in the game at all times.

You need to be smart and tough.

4. CENTRE BACK AND 5. ANOTHER CENTRE BACK

⚽ *Tackling:* **10 (or even 11)**
⚽ *Telepathic communica-tion:* **10**
⚽ *Strength of a pro wrestler:* **10**
⚽ *Heading the ball:* **10**
⚽ *Passing deep:* **8**
⚽ *Dribbling:* **6**
⚽ *Also having nightmares about scoring own goals (mainly with headers):* **1**

A lot of teams these days just line up three **Centre Backs** and they become the last line of defence, or 'stoppers'. However, that's making something incredibly complicated and skilful sound simple. **Centre Backs** not only need to be brilliantly agile – so they can ruin a midfielder's or forward's day by stopping them from scoring show-off goals and looking amazing – they also need to be strong and work together like a machine. Plus they need to be as good in the air as any attacker.

So basically a basketball player, crossed with a rugby forward, who happens to be really good at ballet.

MIDFIELDERS

6. AND 8. CENTRAL MIDFIELD

All-around ability: 10
Being several places at once: 10
Initiative: 10
Long-range shooting: 10
Working hard: 10
Defending (obvs): 10
Spatial awareness of a bat: 10
Stamina of a swallow: 10
Discipline: 10
Speed: 7
Dribbling: 6
Modesty: 2

At home, **Central Midfielders** can probably do complicated algebra, unblock the toilet, bake a cake, put up shelves and teach the dog circus tricks. All at once. On the pitch you're in the thick of the fight: you're defending, making plays, keeping the team's formation, attacking. If football was a fight, a **Central Midfielder** would be the one on a cool horse right in the middle of everything waving a huge axe about ... yelling.

You need to have great tactics, as many of the 'plays' (quick attacking tactics) come from the **Central Midfielder**, but you need to be just as happy defending or passing good balls to the forwards so they can grab all the glory.

It's a position that can be changed into being a **Defensive Midfielder** AKA **Holding Midfielder**, which doesn't mean you're allowed to hold onto anything (ball, nice people's hands, passing attacker's pants). Spoiling attacks with feet that stick to the ball like they've been superglued to the leather is one of the main things you'll need to be able to do.

The main job is to keep the ball a) in the attacking zone (other side's half) and b) out of defending zone (your half).

You also need to be super fit. In any match, a

Central Midfielder can run over seven miles (that's 11km if you're running in Europe). But you also need to have very good all-round vision as you're the glue that binds the team's defence and attack.

If **Central Midfielders** had super powers, you wouldn't need any backs or goalies. Unfortunately not all of us have been genetically modified into invincible soccer robots, so most **Central Midfielders** have to work very hard at skills like tackling, passing and dribbling (with the ball).

7. AND 11. RIGHT MIDFIELDER

⚽ *Ball crossing:* **10**
⚽ *Dribbling:* **10**
⚽ *Duelling with defenders:* **10**
⚽ *Accelerating like a motorbike:* **10**
⚽ *Changing direction:* **8**
⚽ *Fooling defenders:* **8**
⚽ *Staying still for more than a few seconds:* **2**

Sometimes (actually, quite often) known as a **Winger**, they are players who don't mind being on the edge of the game because what they love to do best is sprint down the outside like they're powered on rocket fuel, trick a defender into running the wrong way, and finish up by crossing the ball into the goal area with all the deadly precision, speed and accuracy of a prehistoric terror bird that's just spotted a bunny rabbit.

You need to be patient, because there's not a lot going on for you sometimes, then incredibly quick to react when an opportunity arises. This is because you can be sure that a good **Full Back** will be trying to stop you doing what you enjoy most: that's creating goals or even taking a shot at goal yourself – usually from a tricky angle, which just makes it all the more incredibly satisfying when you score.

'7' is often considered the magic shirt number.

COOL QUOTES

'To be the ultimate team, you must use your body and your mind. Draw upon the resources of your teammates. Choose your steps wisely and you will win. Remember, only teams succeed.'

– Jose Mourinho

FORWARDS

9. STRIKER

- Goal-scoring ability: 10
- Knowledge of the offside rule: 10
- Speed: 10
- Cool head under pressure: 10
- Hilarious goal celebration: 10
- Defending: 6
- Friends with goalies: 2

Strikers come in all shapes and sizes. Frankly, it doesn't matter if you're a little old lady with a shopping trolley, a blob of sentient jelly or a pufferfish – if you can keep a cool head under pressure when (up to) a few million fans are shouting at you and several defenders the size of trolls are trying to run you over and still score a goal, then you're a striker. You'll also need to work on an amazing goal celebration, like a trademark.

Speed onto the ball and precision as you kick or head it are essential, but you also need to have the offside rule tattooed onto your brain with a laser. You can be a 'poacher', a player who positions themselves well forward and doesn't assist the build-up play (otherwise known as a 'goal hanger'); a 'target man' – good for tall players who can win battles in the air against defenders when their 'strike partner' puts the ball up; or a 'deep-lying player', which means you suck defenders away from other players, so they can score instead.

Most likely to be the biggest hero or vilest villain at the end of a game.

10. CENTRE FORWARD

10

⚽ Goal-scoring ability: 10
⚽ Knowledge of the offside rule: 10
⚽ Speed: 10
⚽ Cool head under pressure: 10
⚽ Hilarious goal celebration: 10
⚽ Defending: 8
⚽ Friends with goalies: 2

Yup, you guessed it, the **Centre Forward** is basically another **Striker**. They'll usually have skills the other (or main) **Striker** does not have, for example they are good in the air or skilled at stopping defenders getting their grubby feet on the ball whilst the other attackers get in position. However, when all is said and done, they are there because they can be relied on to get the ball in the back of the net at the slightest opportunity.

Centre Forwards are the humble geniuses we cheer on a freezing afternoon when it feels like your feet have turned to blocks of ice and your hands have gone a worrying shade of blue. But we don't mind because they remind us that football is fantastic.

SOME OTHER POSITIONS

Football is a fast, fluid game and a team manager has lots of options when deciding what positions and formations will be used for that season or even a specific game. This is based on the skills of the players they have, the team they're playing against and what strategy and tactics they want to use (see Chapter 4).

Here are some other possible positions they can choose:

SWEEPER

As the game has become more cunning, **Sweepers** have been invented. To begin with, their job was to stay right back with the defenders and 'sweep' up any loose balls from a tackle, then hoof it up the pitch, as far away from the goal as possible. However, now they're expected to be able to 'play make': this means pass accurately at distance to midfielders or run with the ball up the pitch to form a devastating counter attack, which makes them more like a **Defensive Midfielder**.

ATTACKING MIDFIELDER

The manager might decide that a team's midfield needs more offensive ability (as in attacking ability, not calling out rude names and swearing). An **Attacking Midfielder** will have all the same capability of a normal midfielder but perhaps with better long-range passing and striking skills.

COOL QUOTES

'Many people say I'm the best women's soccer player in the world. I don't think so. And because of that, someday I just might be.'
– Mia Hamm

INSIDE FORWARDS

Basically, this is a **Winger** who won't do what he or she is told. A team will play an **Inside Forward** or **Winger** but never both, as their roles are very similar. The only difference is that an **Inside Forward** won't spend so much time running up and down the touchline like one of those robotic cameras used in big matches. Instead they'll position themselves closer to the centre and be more of a scoring threat.

SECOND STRIKER

We've all been there: the ball goes forward, someone shoots for the goal and it bounces off the crossbar or off someone's face and lands at your feet. Quite a lot of people (author included) would get totally over-excited at this point and kick the ball as hard as they could – right over the goal and into the car park.

But not if you're a **Second Striker**! Before the **Goalkeeper** can scoop it up or the **Full Back** can clear it, you'll take it on the half volley and score. To everyone's huge relief and mad joy.

FASCINATING FACTS

Longest goal in professional football

Newport County's goalkeeper, **Tom King,** scored a goal against Cheltenham in 2021 from his own box. It went an incredible **315 feet** (96.01 metres) before landing in the back of the net of a very surprised goalkeeper, **Joshua Griffiths.**

But Sporting Lisbon defender **Ronny** gets the prize for the **strongest kick,** which has been measured at **221 km per hour** (more than 137 miles per hour). Scary.

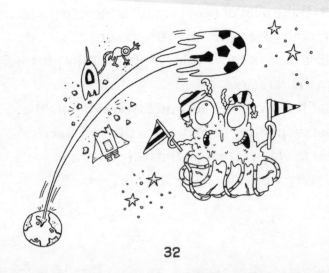

A FUNNY THING HAPPENED

Any player who manages to score four goals in the same match would normally be thrilled with their achievement – as would all the fans, the rest of the team and their mum.

Unfortunately for Aston Villa defender, Chris Nicholl, two of the four goals he scored on 20th March 1976 were own goals for Leicester City. To make his mistakes all the more obvious, he was the only person who scored in the entire ninety minutes – the match finishing in a 2-2 draw. That said, giving an interview after the match, he seemed pretty cheerful.

'The third goal, Leicester's second, was a cracker. Best goal I ever scored. A diving header. No goalkeeper would have saved that. Fortunately my fourth equalised for [Aston] Villa, so that was a relief.'

RONALDO

If robot geniuses were to design a goal-scoring machine, it would probably look and act quite like Cristiano Ronaldo, but perhaps without quite so much spitting.

Already the top goal scorer of all time (see page 99), it's just possible the Portuguese player might end his career on 1000 professional goals. Unbelievable.

So how does he do it?

REALLY HARD WORK

Sorry but it's true. Ronaldo is probably the hardest-working player on the planet — even at 37 (pretty ancient for a footballer), he can jump higher than a lot of basketball players (FACT) and has the physical strength to muscle past the toughest defenders. He's got an eight pack and legs like a pit pony.

MENTAL STRENGTH

But having a gym membership card is not enough ... again, in spite of his successes, he is super competitive and is STILL pushing himself to the limit every time he goes out on the pitch.

SMART

He's always been clever enough to know that having great kicking and dribbling skills is not enough: Ronaldo not only learns from the (few) mistakes he makes but has always said his main goal when he goes out on the pitch (apart from the actual goal), is to ENJOY HIMSELF.

Success and self-belief might make him seem a little big headed at times but if anyone deserves to think they're a FOOTBALL SUPER CYBORG, it's Ronaldo.

CHAPTER 3:
THE MATCH

The Pitch

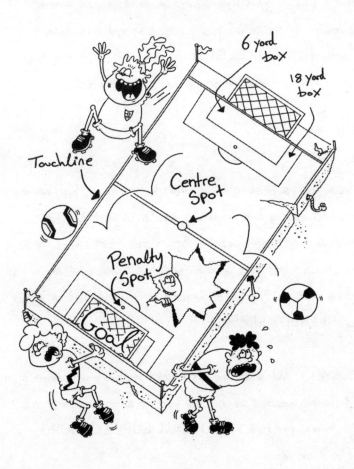

As we all know, you can play football just about anywhere: on grass, Astro turf, tarmac, bare earth, in stadiums with hundreds of thousands of spectators, in streets, playgrounds, ballparks, on beaches, in corridors and courtyards.

Football doesn't get too stressed about making everything exactly the same all the time, every time. **The International Football Association Board** (IFAB), which writes the rules of soccer, says that a professional pitch can be anything from 50 to 100 yards in width and 100 to 130 yards in length.

This extreme flexibility is one of the best things about football and has helped it become such a stupendously popular game: for example the grounds at Fulham (Craven Cottage), Crystal Palace (Selhurst Park) and Liverpool (Anfield) are all five or six yards shorter than most.

I once played on a flat roof overlooking London. Very carefully.

And, while we're on the subject of regulation sizes, even the ball doesn't have to be exactly the same every time in a professional match. Wikipedia – that knows everything – states:

'Regulation size and weight for a soccer ball is a circumference of 68–70 cm and a weight of between 410–450g. The ball should be inflated to a pressure of 0.6 and 1.1 bars (8.7 and 16.0 psi) at sea level. This is known as Size 5.'

So, there you go.

Most other sports require equipment you don't need for anything else, for instance:

Swimming – goggles, type of stretchy underwear you wouldn't normally be seen dead in, and nothing to make you sink (eg suit of armour),

Tennis – racket, quite a lot of balls,

Skiing – skis, polar-bear-proof clothing,

Sky diving – a plane and at least one parachute. Two's better.

And a special place to compete:

Swimming – water (more than a bathful),

Tennis – no hills, or deep holes, and a

net,
Skiing – several handy mountains next door to each other,
Sky diving – empty sky, no active volcanoes.

But as long as you have something vaguely round and you're not, say, strapped to a parachute half a mile up in mid-air, you have a good chance of finding somewhere suitable for a bit of a kickabout.

SCORING

Is ridiculously simple.

In theory: you score a goal (worth one point) by putting the ball 'in the back of the net', that is to say: it needs to go between the goalposts, underneath the crossbar and behind the goal line. And, as long as you don't use your hands, or anything mechanical (like a trebuchet or a rocket launcher), it's a goal.

And everyone cheers.

In practice, it's a lot harder than that because you've got several people trying their hardest to stop you scoring a goal, which is why boys and girls starting football have to learn to work as a team.

Goals can be scored in five types of action:

- ⚽ **A shot at goal** in open play (from anywhere on the pitch, by any player).
- ⚽ **A free kick**, after a foul committed outside the box.
- ⚽ **Penalty kick**, after a foul committed in the box.
- ⚽ **A corner kick**, when the ball has been put behind the goal line by the defending team.
- ⚽ **Penalty shoot-out** after extra time, in a match where there has to be a winner.

Note: A goal cannot be scored directly from a throw-in. If the ball enters the opponent's goal, a goal kick is awarded. If the ball enters the thrower's goal, a corner kick is awarded.

How long is a game of soccer?

In 1866 London and Sheffield were warming up to play each other. Up until then, football matches varied in length according to:

⚽ **What** both teams decided was a good length of time for a decent game.
⚽ **How** fit the teams were.
⚽ **When** it was dinnertime.

On that day, for whatever reason, both **London** and **Sheffield** captains shook hands and decided to play for **ninety minutes** and, for some reason, that just stuck. And not just for those two sides, but for every other professional side, in **any** match **anywhere** in the world. **Forever**.

On top of the **ninety minutes** of play, there is a **fifteen-minute** break at half time to get your breath back, eat half an orange and be shouted out by the coach. Plus 'stoppage time' for injuries, substitutions and people running onto the pitch waving underwear in the air.

There are, of course, a few exceptions to this ninety-minute time limit, especially as the game develops.

1. If extra time is needed: thirty minutes is added on, with a change of ends halfway through.
2. Paralympic matches can be anything from thirty minutes to an hour long.
3. Different format games, like five-a-side will be under ninety minutes – usually around fifty to sixty minutes, or less.

PENALTIES AND FREE KICKS

Let's start with penalties. These are given to the other side when a defending player fouls an attacking player or uses his or her hands in the **penalty area**, otherwise known as the box. When this happens, the defending side and all their supporters shout at the referee and generally complain to anyone who'll listen about how unfair it all is. And everyone on the attacking team, which now has an easy-ish shot at goal, thinks the ref is amazingly clever, the most fantastic person who ever lived and they all want to invite them on holiday.

When the penalty is taken, the ball is placed by the kicker on the **penalty spot**. The goalkeeper can move sideways, left and right, but they can't move off the goal line until the shot is taken.

It's one-on-one and quite scary for both the kicker and the goalkeeper. Probably a bit more terrifying for the kicker as all of us watching think it's easy in our heads – unless it's actually us that has to take the penalty in front of all our friends and mortal enemies. In which case, the goalmouth shrinks to the size of a toilet cubicle and our feet feel like they've turned into lumps of wet earth.

Just remember to breathe ... and that you're stronger than you think.

A **free kick**, on the other hand, is when a crime against the laws of football and fair play is committed outside the penalty area. A free kick can be direct or indirect. A direct free kick can be shot at goal and indirect kick must touch another player before it goes in the goal. For both kicks the ball must be on the ground and not moving before the kick is taken. It's a great opportunity to show off curling the ball (if you can).

WHAT'S A FOUL EXACTLY?

To be honest, I wish you'd never asked; it's rather complicated. But here goes...

There are **three** basic ways you can get into trouble in football: the first is doing something physically wrong – tripping another player up, hurting them, or putting them in danger; the second is unsporting behaviour – not respecting the referee, other players, swearing, stopping play for no reason; and the third is breaking the rules – using your hands, playing before the referee says you can, riding about the penalty area on a horse.

If a foul is really bad (usually dangerous), the player will get a **yellow card**, if they get two yellow cards in one match or if what they have done is worse than really bad, they'll get given a **red card** and sent off the pitch. Then your side will be down to ten players and will probably lose. And it will be all your fault.

COOL QUOTES

'Everything happens for a reason if you work hard for it.'
– Julie Ertz

The actual list of fouls is huge and, if I tried to write them all down, there wouldn't be much space in this book left for fun stuff like jokes or Matt's cartoons. You can look them up but most of the time you'll know when you've done something wrong – and if you don't, the referee will tell you immediately (as well as all the mums and dads supporting the other team).

THROW-INS

Are great fun. You get a **throw-in** when the ball is kicked over the **touchline** (the lines down the side of the pitch) by someone on the other side. When taking a throw-in just remember you have to let go of the ball with both hands at the same time and you have to have your feet on the ground when you do, otherwise the throw-in is called 'foul' and goes to the other team.

CORNERS

The corner is one of the most exciting parts of
any football game, when anything can happen
– mainly because there are loads of players
crowding the goal area, jostling each
other for a good position as the ball
curls through the air like a comet.
A corner is given when the
ball goes out of bounds
behind the goal. Again,
being accurate and able
to curl the ball is a very
useful skill to have.
An attacking side can
score from a corner.

OFFSIDE

When an **attacking** player has the ball passed to them in the other team's half, they cannot be in front of the last defender.

Knowing the offside rule in football is one of those things grown-ups and friends will use to check if you really know anything about football. So, if you learn this off by heart, it will impress anyone ... or at least keep them quiet.

But this is a tricky rule. You can be in an offside position but not get in trouble if you don't become involved in active play. There's a handy acronym, PIG (**plays**, **interferes** or **gains** an advantage) to describe becoming involved in active play and therefore committing an offside offence.

However, knowing a rule and actually understanding it is very different, so my advice to you is look at these diagrams, then go online and look at loads of videos of players getting whistled at by the ref for offside.

Be careful you're not doing this instead of homework. Although it is homework. **Fact.**

COOL QUOTES

'I'm lucky to be part of a team who help to make me look good, and they deserve as much of the credit for my success as I do for the hard work we have all put in on the training ground.'

– Lionel Messi

FASCINATING FACT

Longest Penalty Shoot-out
A total of **54** spot-kicks were needed to separate winning team Washington FC from Bedlington Terriers in a shootout which eventually finished **25-24**.

Amazingly, there were more penalties taken during the match, than there were fans attending.

A FUNNY THING HAPPENED...

It's every football fan's dream to jog out into a huge stadium with some of the best players in the world.

On the night of 18 April 2001, at Bayern Munich's Olympic Stadium, Karl Power, an unemployed labourer from Greater Manchester, somehow managed to dodge security.

Moments later, he strolled out with the Manchester United team, before cheekily posing alongside the likes of Dwight Yorke, Ryan Giggs and Fabian Barthez for the official team picture.

JAMIE TREGASKISS

Since he had been a small kid, Jamie had wanted to play professional football. Things seemed to be going pretty well on that front when, aged just ten, he was scouted by his favourite club, **MANCHESTER CITY**.

But, by 13, he was **FINISHED**.

Jamie had his left leg amputated after pain in his hip turned out to be a rare form of bone cancer. He had no choice: it was either **HIS LEG OR HIS LIFE**. And that was the end of his football dream. Or so everyone thought...

But there is no stopping some people! With just one leg (and two crutches), Jamie worked like the sports demon he is to hone his natural skills as a player. And so, at twenty-five, he has become one of the best amputee footballers in the world. Even better, he did get to play for Manchester City FC (still does) — not only that, he plays for his country as a GREAT BRITAIN AND ENGLAND AMPUTEE.

And, if you're thinking, well, yeah but one-legged footballers might be ok against other disabled players, but who'd watch it? just go online at search up 'JAMIE TREGASKISS GOAL ALL EVENT SWITZERLAND', or any amputee football skills vids.

You'll be glad you did.

CHAPTER 4:
SKILLS AND TACTICS

If people didn't get tackled, there wouldn't be much point in watching football half the time. But tackling effectively, so you don't get sent off for an early shower, is tricky ... here are some helpful tips.

The first thing to know is that a **tackler** must always play the ball, and not charge into the player like an angry ostrich, then start biting his ankles until he gives you the ball. That's called rugby.

Most people are happy to accept that there are **three types** of basic tackle in football.

THE BLOCK TACKLE
THE POKE TACKLE
THE SLIDE TACKLE

For all of them, the aim is to stop the attacking player doing what they want to do, which includes passing it to another player on their team or – better still – waltzing through your defence and scoring impressively.

On top of that, it would be even better if the tackle ended up with you getting the ball and doing all sorts of fun and amusing things with it instead.

Make sure you have your feet planted firmly on the ground (for balance) and don't rush the attacking player. Instead, watch where they are going: a good way to do this is watch the direction their hips are facing, not where they are looking as that could be a trick. And look out for a shot or a **pass**, as this is what **block tackling** is best at stopping.

As the attacker runs out of ways to escape, close in and make sure you have most of your body weight behind the foot you are using to block the ball with. That way, you are less likely to fall over when you make contact with the ball and with the attacker.

Aim to block the middle of the ball and lock your knees and ankles for added strength.

You've just made yourself into a miniature fortress – a bit like Gandalf in *The Lord of the Rings* when he tells the Balrog (large evil spirit), '**You shall not pass.**'*

*NOTE *Although they weren't playing football at the time.*

POKE TACKLE

Instead of blocking the ball, this type of tackle aims to get the ball away from the player with a crafty, jabbing (or poking) kick. If you're quicker than the player you have just tackled, you will be able to gain possession of the ball by scampering after it. However, most often with this type of tackle, the ball either goes out or goes to another player (hopefully one on your team).

It's very good for **slowing down** an attack so your team can regroup.

Unlike the block tackle, you should approach the player from the side or behind.

Watch the ball and the player's legs or feet like a cat stares at a budgie in a cage (except don't lick your lips or you'll look weird).

When the player and the ball are close enough,

use your foot nearest the ball to 'stab' it away from the player with the tip of your boot.

SLIDE TACKLE

If you do this properly, it makes you look like a **football genius**. If you do it wrong, you'll either look like you've run up to another player and attacked them with your feet (and possibly get sent off) or you'll miss them completely and slide right past them on your bottom with a surprised look on your face.

However, as long as you think you are fast enough and you can see space between the attacker and the ball, it's worth giving this a go once in a while because giving things a go is what makes sport fun.

So, use your leg farthest from the ball and bend the other leg under your butt. Then slide (with deadly grace) on your hip towards the tackle. It's best to make contact with the centre or the top half of the ball to hook it in the opposite direction in order to keep it or knock it out of play.

PASSING

The Three Types of Pass

People say there is only back, forward and square passing.

But that does sound very boring.

Then again, folk who jump up and down on the spot and swear that there are loads more types of passes are possibly people who just like making lists of things.

So, we at **Stupendous Sports** are going to come up with a nice, reasonable compromise and say you can easily have lots of fun playing football knowing about six types of pass.

Long Pass

Usually sent from a Defender or Defensive Midfielder, these passes will travel the furthest (most often to a forward attacking player) and they need the most power and accuracy. Often called a **'long ball'**.

Through Pass

You've got two players in front of you and a gap between them. Out of the corner of your eye, you see one of your mates running across the pitch. If you time it perfectly (and you will, with practice), you can slot the ball between the two defending players, so your attacking player can get onto the ball and into a scoring position. Often called a **'through ball'**.

Cross

This is usually another long-ish pass but, instead of passing up the field, you pass from around the sidelines, into the attacking area (penalty box). Again, you need to be accurate, often because you're running as you pass.

Give and go

This is very similar to the one-touch pass, sometimes called a **One-Two**. It's kind of treating your teammate like a wall in five-a-side. So, you pass to them, run into space behind the defenders, and they one touch pass the ball back to you. Boom!

Backheel

Probably the most impressive pass (or the daftest) because – most of the time – you are not looking where you pass. Instead, you kick the ball backwards with your heel to someone you know (or very much hope) is just behind you. Professional footballers love to do this.

A HANDY NOTE ON INTERCEPTS

You simply can't talk about passing without mentioning their deadly enemy: **the Intercept**.

Instead of tackling, some players are very good and exceedingly crafty at spotting when an attacking player is about to pass the ball. It helps if you're very good at snooker or geometry, because you can '**see**' an invisible line of dots going from the player with the ball towards the one you think they are going to pass to.

All you need to do then is run to the nearest point of that line, scoop up the ball and dribble away cackling madly.

Brilliant ... and there's no chance of fouling anyone.

ANOTHER NOTE ON INTERCEPTS

Some types of football (**walking football** or French five-a-side) don't allow tackling, so the only way to gain possession of a ball is through an intercept. Excellent training.

DRIBBLING

As we all know dribbling can mean one of two things these days:

1. To spill food/drink out of your mouth by not closing it properly = everyone avoids you.

2. To move skilfully about a pitch or court with a ball in your **possession** = you avoid everyone.

In fact it comes from one very old word, **drib** (verb), which means to trickle, or move carefully.

And that just about sums it up for soccer, in that dribbling is all about the very important skill of pushing the ball along the ground with your feet and not losing it to another player. The only thing that's changed is you don't so much move along slowly ('**trickle**') as race down the wing like a rocket, shimmy around several defenders and shoot the ball into the goal. Or, at least you would if your name is Messi, Maradona or Pelé.

Or, in fact, any of the great players, because dribbling is one of those skills you have to have if you want to be considered OK at football. Some people say it is at the very heart of what makes football such a great game.

COOL QUOTES

**'Football is about joy.
It's about dribbling.'**
– Ronaldinho

There are three (maybe four) reasons why you would risk dribbling in football – instead of just passing it to a teammate:

1. Getting away from pressure (defenders closing in on you).
2. Running at players to beat them.
3. Freeing up space to pass.
4. ... generally showing off.

There are loads of techniques and training **exercises** you can do to improve these skills but they boil down to you being able to keep the ball at your feet and move along fast while still keeping an eye on your enemies.

HERE ARE SOME TIPS:

⚽ Practise running in a straight line with the ball, using both the inside and the outside of your feet.

⚽ Now try changing direction as much as possible, as you run along.

⚽ Then change your speed (fast, slow, medium, etc).

⚽ Practise glancing up every so often but keep moving.

⚽ Have a go at '**propelling**' the ball a bit ahead of you (but not too far – about a metre) as if popping it past a player, charging round them and carrying on to goals and glory.

There's plenty of other stuff you can do as you get better (see **Useful Tricks** p73) but this should be enough to beat your brother and amaze your friends.

FOOTBALL FORMATIONS

Really super simply put, formations are all about where to put your players so that you stand the best chance of winning.

Choice of **formation** can be down to:

⚽ The skills your different players have.
⚽ The formation the other side is using.
⚽ Whether you want to defend (because you've already scored).
⚽ ... or attack (because they've scored and you need to).

Most formations have names which are just numbers that show how many attackers there will be compared to defenders (and midfielders). Sometimes they will have cool names.

Some examples of **fantastic football formations**:

2-3-5 (or '**Pyramid**')

Looks like a pyramid and is solid like one, too, because it's a nice, even mix of attacking, midfield and defensive players. It gave football its shirt numbering system and was popular from **1880** in England where it spread to the rest of the world. It was used by teams like Uruguay to win the **FIFA World Cup** in 1930.

4-4-2

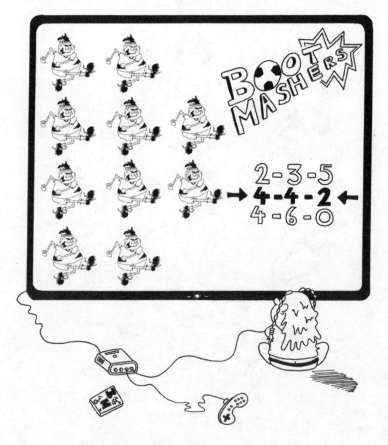

Probably the most popular formation in modern football.

4-6-0

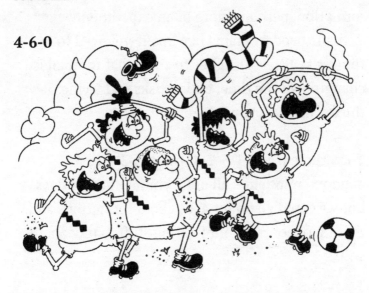

'What no **Striker**?' you cry out while you eat your dinner, spraying bits of spaghetti hoop all over your dad.

'Yes, son,' he says, removing a turkey twizzler from his eyebrow. 'But all those fast attackers running about – every one of whom can score – are very hard for defenders to mark without moving out of their formation. This,' he says, raising his finger in the air like he's about to tell you there's a big bag of diamonds or a chest full of chocolate hidden in the garden, 'is the future of football!'

'OK, Dad,' you say, not so sure, as you go back to

this amazing book and wonder what's for pudding. But your dad's right (for once. It is a very weird formation, perhaps more of an experiment. Actually used by teams like Spain (referred to as the '**False 9**'), it just goes to show that football is changing all the time, taking risks and trying new things, which is why we all love it.

Then there is the **4-3-2-1**, the **4-2-3-1** or a diamond midfield – all quite common these days. But we could go on for ages about formations and there's lots of other interesting stuff to talk about still.

PLAYING STYLES

You could say that football is like chess, but on a very big board and without any players that look like horses. **Tactics** (planning and thinking) are just as important in football as in chess and that's why, if you watch or play enough soccer, you'll often hear about playing styles.

So it's useful to know what your mates or the coach are going on about.

Here's a (very) quick guide.

Core (or main) style of play:

1. **Attacking** (trying to score).
2. **Defending** (trying to stop the other side scoring).

... so far, so easy-peasy, but it gets more cunning than this. Here goes:

ATTACKING STYLES

There's a simple way to look at this, which should be fine for most of us, unless you are suddenly taken out of double maths to play in the **Premier League**.

1. DIRECT ATTACK

This is where the defence is using **long passes** and **through balls**, often in the air, to get the ball to the players right up front.

Advantage

It can get the ball into scoring range very quickly. And it's exciting to watch.

Disadvantage

A lot of these types of passes are **intercepted** or 'challenged' by the defending team, so you can lose possession and be on the end of a lightning counter-attack.

2. INDIRECT ATTACK

Sometimes called the **Possession Style**, which uses lots of short passes (forwards, mainly, but sideways and backwards, too), looking for weaknesses in the other side. Defenders can be moved up and down to help with an attack (called **Pushing Up**) or can defend deep.

Advantage

You keep possession of the ball more easily.

Disadvantage

Harder than it looks and you can go a long time without scoring, so not great if you're running out of time in a game.

DEFENDING STYLES

1. One-to-one or man marking
Where players are marked by other players individually.

2. Zone Defence
Where each player defends an area of the pitch rather than marking another individual. AKA 'Zonal marking'.

Other modern styles

TOTAL FOOTBALL

The Netherlands came up with total football, the greatest tactical innovation in the history of soccer. The concept of total football was that every player can play in any position as long as the formation remains the same.

Gegenpressing

Literally meaning '**press against**' but often translated as counter-pressing, this style of football originated in Germany and basically means that as soon as the opposition gets the ball you should run at them and pester them so that they can't think straight about what to do with it, and so you are able to win the ball back quickly.

Some Traditional National Playing Styles

It's interesting that many countries are famous for playing in particular ways. Here are just a few examples.

English Style

Oldest style there is (not surprisingly). Attacks are set up quickly and balls passed deep, missing out midfielders.

Italian Style

Careful and slow. Defenders hang back and keep things calm, attackers **creep** up, often coming at the goal from the sides.

Brazilian Style

Said to have originated in street football, the Brazilians' ball skills allow for lots of passing and dribbling, very **quick** and **fluid**. Great to watch because things (good or bad) can happen very quickly.

German Style

Very structured, formations are rigid and the other team is put under pressure by placing lots of attackers near the goal. Sometimes not that great to watch but very effective. In any case, they often go in for 'Gegenpressing' these days (see p71).

Spanish Style

Fluid build-up play. Lots of triangular passing (called **Tiki-Taka**).

Don't forget, national teams and national leagues borrow styles all the time to suit their tactics.

Useful Tricks

As you get better at football and you begin to feel confident with the basics – like passing, dribbling, tackling and putting your shorts on the right way round – you are going to start to think about learning a few tricks to impress everyone.

This can be scary because if a trick doesn't go right, it can only go wrong. That is to say, if a game of keepy-uppy goes wrong, you won't get away with pretending you always meant to trip over your shoelaces and fall backwards into a hedge.

But, if you can practise quietly (in your back garden, with no one looking), chances are you'll soon get confident enough to pull a few **stunts** in front of your mates.

KEEPY-UPPY

This won't win matches but it will improve your ball skills and it looks pretty impressive. Sometimes called '**kick-ups**'.

It's basically juggling a ball with your feet, knees, head or even shoulders. You can do it on your own or with friends and family.

How:

⚽ Start by using your stronger foot (usually the right) to flick the ball up, then kick it up to around waist height, so you can catch it. Keep repeating this until you get comfortable doing this every time.

⚽ Now try this with your other foot. It will take a bit longer, but you'll get there eventually.

⚽ Now try both feet – one after the other. Once you get that, instead of catching the ball, let it drop back down to your feet and then kick it back up.

⚽ Keep doing this in your back garden until it gets dark and everyone wonders where you are.

⚽ Repeat every night for a week after school and you'll soon be a keepy-uppy **Jedi Master**.

For a fantastic example of this type of ball control, type in '**Maradona's pre-match warm-up**' anywhere on the internet. You won't regret it.

CRUYFF TURN

OK, let's try and keep this as simple as possible:

1. Keep your back to the person who is trying to get the ball off you.
2. Pretend to pass the ball with (let's say) your right foot by making out you are kicking it forwards.
3. But, instead, tap it backwards and turn to follow it.
4. The player trying to get the ball off you will nearly always think you're passing the ball one way and run after it, as you shoot off the other way, grinning from ear to ear.

This trick sounds like a hairstyle, but it's not. It's called the Cruyff Turn after the great Dutch player, Johan Cruyff, who invented the move (as well as being brilliant at almost everything else in football).

Watch it online (**Hal Robson-Kanu** does a great one, as well as Cruyff himself obviously), then practise with a friend, so you can fool your enemies.

SCORPION KICK

Dada?

As the above shows, dive forward onto your hands and attempt to kick the ball with your feet behind your head as the ball comes towards you. Timing is everything. Your feet coming over your head and hitting the ball will either look like a scorpion's tail **stinger** or like the world's worst handstand. If you do it wrong, you'll basically end up kicking yourself in the butt in front of all your friends.

Probably best to try and get the hang of this with a nice soft gym mat nearby or even beside a swimming pool.

Super hard, completely useless but really impressive – so why not!

When Colombia played England at Wembley in 1995, the South American nation's goalkeeper **Rene Higuita** wrote himself into footballing history by coming up with a scorpion-kick save. Take a look.

SCISSOR KICK AND/ OR BICYCLE KICK

Incredibly impressive way to kick the ball, even more impressive way to score.

1. Keep your eye on the ball.

2. Jump using the leg that you kick with, while also bringing your other leg off the ground.

3. Let yourself fall backwards (for a bicycle kick) or sideways (for a scissor kick) while in the air.

3. Before you hit the ground, use your kicking leg to kick at the ball, and bring your other leg down.

4. Try to use your hands and arms to slow your fall.

6. Soak up the applause, run for **president** next week.

NOTE It's a good idea to make sure you do it on a nice soggy pitch or wear pads!

Wayne Rooney, Christiano Ronaldo and Zlatan Ibramović have scored some of the best goals ever this way.

'I've never scored a goal in my life without getting a pass from someone else.'

– Abby Wambach

FASCINATING FACT

Longest header

The longest header is measured at just over **190 feet** by Norway's **Jone Samuelsen** who redirected a **blasted header** in the opposite direction and bounced it into the net to secure a win in **2011** against **Tromsø.**

A FUNNY THING HAPPENED...

In 2011, Manchester City striker Mario Balotelli went to a school to tell off a headmaster. A young fan asked Balotelli for an autograph at training, and the Italian asked why he wasn't at school. The fan told his football hero he was being bullied, at which point Balotelli went straight to the school with the boy and his mother and demanded to see the headmaster to sort things out.

MEGAN RAPINOE

Is a soccer star in anyone's book (including this one). In a career lasting over a decade, she has probably ended up with one of the most impressive downstairs loos on the planet, with two Olympic medals hanging up, a Golden Boot (top goal scorer) at the 2019 WORLD CUP and the Golden Ball award for being the top player in the tournament. She has also been named FIFA'S WOMEN'S WORLD PLAYER OF THE YEAR 2019.

Megan is most effective/famous for playing on the wing and her style of football has been described as 'CRAFTY': intelligent crosses that set up goals for other people, more often than actually scoring them herself. She is also very good at varying her pace — she knows that you don't need to do everything at one hundred miles an hour, that sometimes you can trick people by slowing things down ... then speeding up.

One of the players who has changed the face of women's football and also the perception and popularity of football in the USA. She is one of those players helping to show the a world full of young players that anyone can play regardless of where you are from and who you are.

In 2020 she was named as one of *TIME MAGAZINE'S* top one hundred most influential people.

CHAPTER 5:
FUTURE OF THE GAME

Football is fast, fun … and for everyone!

It is played by young people, old people, in-the-middle people. Rich-as-a-king people, poor-as-a-mouse people, men, women, boys and girls...
Perhaps its biggest success, recently, has been the growth in the women's game.

Women's football is now considered to be one of

the fastest-growing sports in the world and, what's more, it's speeding up, with the women's game due to double in size over the next fifteen to twenty years. It might well become the biggest female sport in the USA.

Check these facts out:

Football is the top most played, most watched (most argued about) sport in a whopping **226 countries and dependencies** on planet Earth.

In fact, there are only 35 countries where soccer doesn't make number 1. They are:

American Football

USA

Cricket

Guyana, Antigua and Barbuda, Barbados, Trinidad and Tobago, India, Pakistan, Bangladesh, Sri Lanka, and Australia

Rugby

Fiji, Samoa, Tonga, New Zealand, and Wales

Baseball

Panama, Venezuela, Cuba, The Dominican Republic, Japan, Nicaragua, Puerto Rico, The Northern Marianas and Taiwan

Basketball

The Philippines, Lithuania, Estonia, Marshall Islands, and the Bahamas

Gaelic football

Republic of Ireland

Ice hockey

Canada, Finland and Latvia

Archery

Bhutan

... and **Wrestling**
Mongolia

The football World Cup is the biggest sporting event on earth. When the **FIFA World Cup** is on, it stops the planet: it is three times bigger than the Olympic Games in viewership.

Football Variations

But it doesn't end there: these days there are more different types of football than there are variations on any other sport.

We've got:

BEACH FOOTBALL

Doesn't have to be played at the actual seaside –
any place with sand will do, except, perhaps **Death
Valley**, as it can get a bit hot and they don't have
vending machines in the desert for after-match
drinks.

Beach soccer has pretty much the same rules as
five-a-side. A lot of the pitch lines are imaginary,
as you can't draw straight lines on sand that last
more than a couple of minutes. It originally started
in Brazil as a good way of getting people together
in a friendly way (they have a LOT of beaches in
Brazil).

Beach football has been made more popular still
by big players such as Eric Cantona or Neymar
joining in. It even has its own international
tournaments run by **FIFA** now.

FUTSAL

This is just like the
indoor five-a-side
your dad plays
as an excuse to
go and drink beer
and eat pizza once a
week, except it is very
fast, very skilful and

there aren't any handy walls to bounce the ball off or lean on for a rest. It was originally started in the 1930s by a teacher in **Uruguay** called Juan Carlos Ceriani, as an excuse to play on basketball courts. YMCAs (cheap hotels for young people) made the game popular all across America and, like Beach Football, it has its own national and international competitions.

Even if you play only once in a while, it's a great way to practise your ball control and passing.

In Hong Kong they play it on **rooftops**.

FREESTYLE SOCCER

This is a good example of taking one exciting side of the sport (ball control and tricks) and turning it into a sport all of its own. All you need is a ball and, er ... that's it.

Freestyle is all about juggling the ball and controlling it with your feet, hands, legs, head – any part of your body, really. Music is often played to add to the performance.

To begin with, it wasn't taken very seriously, then top international players like Maradona and Ronaldinho got in on it and everyone decided they loved it from then on. Probably the greatest player is Mr Woo of South Korea who holds several **Guinness World Records** in the sport and has also performed at FIFA World Cup ceremonies.

Partly football, partly dance, partly acrobatics and (a great big) partly showing off.

POWERCHAIR FOOTBALL

For sportspeople with disabilities, it's very like association football except you use a chair to get around and 'kick' the ball. Wheelchairs can be powered (then it's called **Powerchair Football**, obvs), or they can be pushed around by someone else – although the person pushing cannot help in any way by joining in the actual game.

Official matches played (you guessed it) on a basketball court.

BLIND FOOTBALL

This is **Futsal**, except all the players are visually impaired and also blindfolded to make sure no one can see anything at all. Not a thing.

It sounds like it's never going to work, when you explain it but, the players are brilliant and the matches are very exciting (just watch the **Paralympics** or the World Championships). Brazil and Argentina are just about the best – so, actually, it's exactly like association football!

The ball tinkles when it is kicked (makes a noise – not the other type of tinkle), so the players know where it is and, to stop any nasty accidents, the players shout 'voy' or 'go' when they are going for the ball, so other players know where they are and don't crash into them.

Unlike in sighted football, the crowd has to keep completely quiet, so the footballers can concentrate one hundred per cent on the ball and what their opponents and teammates are doing.

The players are **brilliant and brave** and watching it makes you proud of football ... and proud to be a human being.

IMPORTANT NOTE: *Also gaining in popularity is deaf football, pan-disability football, frame football... if you're interested in finding out more go to* ***https://www. englandfootball.com/play/disability-football***

Diversity

But, very sadly, football hasn't always been so welcoming and so diverse.

Almost as soon as it was invented hundreds and hundreds of years ago, people seem to have been trying to stop other people from playing it. It was banned in Scotland for a couple of hundred years (which was mostly ignored) and, in 1921, the FA banned women from playing football on its grounds for fifty years for being 'quite unsuitable for female players'! Even though, just after the First World War, the women's game attracted the biggest crowds (see p12).

Even these days, racism and violence have spoiled matches that, for many, were one of the highlights of their week.

But this seems to be changing. Racist chants on the stands and racist language on social media are punished severely and violent fans (and players) are banned from the sport.

Spirit of the game

Players and fans like you hold the future of this **great sport** in your hands. With the internet and massive TV coverage, supporters know the eyes of the world are on them. And players know that that fans – especially **younger fans** – look up to them and copy what they do: so good behaviour on and off the pitch is becoming more important to how popular a player will be. And more popular means more supporters for the game and more players doing the right thing: making football a giant amongst all other sports, and an inspiration for so many people from every country, colour and creed, even better. Hopefully.

FASCINATING FACTS

Longest Unbeaten Run

Arsenal's Invincibles of 2003-04, were pretty amazing. They rattled off **forty-nine** consecutive unbeaten games, including all thirty-eight games of the **Premier League** season in **2003-04**. The run actually spanned three seasons — the last two games of the 2002-03 season through the first ten games of the 2004-2005 season.

The real unbeatability crown, however, belongs to **Steaua Bucharest**. In the **1980s** the Romanian club terrorized Divizia A with five unbeaten seasons in a row for a **104-game** unbeaten streak.

A(N) ~~FUNNY~~ AMAZING THING HAPPENED ...

And no book about football could be complete without the story of the First World War football match on Christmas Day 1914.

In August 1914 most people thought war would be over by Christmas but when, as a freezing winter took hold, that seemed unlikely to happen, soldiers on both the German and English sides decided to make the best of things and try to celebrate Christmas Eve in spite of the cold, mud and danger.

Pretty soon, they were shouting jokes between the trenches and someone suggested that they had a ceasefire. Everyone agreed it was a good idea and the next morning, on Christmas Day, German and English soldiers clambered out of their muddy trenches all along the line to meet, swap presents and show off pictures of their families.

In one place a football appeared – though what a football was doing in the middle of a war, no one has ever been able to explain – and a game started.

And so, for a short while, they tried and perhaps they succeeded to forget about that terrible war. It was a sort of miracle on Christmas Day and was thanks, in part, to football.

The Germans won on penalties.

COOL QUOTES

'I know, firsthand that soccer brings people together - all it takes is a ball and a few people, and the seeds of friendship are planted.

– Ali Krieger

PELÉ

No spotlight on players could be complete without including Pelé.

Possibly the first world wide football super star, he won an amazing three **WORLD CUPS** for Brazil, two **WORLD CHAMPIONSHIPS** and scored over 1000 first class goals in his career (not all in professional games, so he is not the world record holder).

Whilst he was considered the best player for almost every side he ever played for, he had a reputation for being the member of the team that bought everyone together, which is as important as being a soccer JEDI genius.

Pelé's electrifying play and the way he turned goal scoring into a spectacular art made him a star around the world. Amazingly, in 1967, in Nigeria, a 48-hour cease-fire in that nation's civil war was called to allow all to watch the great player do his stuff. **WHAT OTHER SPORT STOPS WARS?**

Pelé got the International Peace Award in 1978. In 1980 he was named **ATHLETE OF THE CENTURY** by the French sports magazine L'Equipe, and he received the same honour in 1999 from the **INTERNATIONAL OLYMPIC COMMITTEE.**

Random Fun Fact: Pelé was named after American inventor Thomas Edison, his real name being Edson Arantes do Nascimiento.

NOTE. Correct at time of writing

FASCINATING STATS

Top ten professional goalscorers, men

10. **Tulio Maravilha**
575 goals (total games unknown) – **1988-2019**

9. **Uwe Seeler**
575+ goals (total games unknown) – **1953-1978**

8. **Ferenc Deak**
576+ goals (total games unknown) – **1940-1957**

7. **Gerd Muller**
734 goals in **793** games – **1962-1981**

6. **Ferenc Puskas**
746+ goals in **754+** games – **1943-1966**

5. **Lionel Messi**

769 goals in **974** games – **2003-present**

4. **Pelé**

757+ goals in **831** games – **1957-1977**

3. **Romario**

772 goals **994** games – **1985-2007**

2. **Josef Bican**

805+ goals in **530+** games – **1931-1956**

1. **Cristiano Ronaldo**

815 goals in **1121** games – **2001-present**

Top International goalscorers, women

1. **Christine Sinclair** (Canada) **189** goals in **310** games

2. **Abby Wombach** (USA) **184** goals **255** games

3. **Mia Hamm** (USA) **158** goals in **275** games

4. **Birgit Prinz** (Germany) **128** goals in **214** games

5. **Julie Fleeting** (Scotland) **116** goals in **121** games

6. **Maysa Jbarah** (Jordan) **113** goals in **110** games

7. **Patrizia Panico** (Italy) **110** goals in **204** games

8. **Marta** (Brazil) **109** goals in **155** games

9. **Sun Wen** (China PR) **106** goals in **152** games

10. **Portia Modise** (South Africa) **101** goals in **124** games

FASCINATING FACT

However, special mention should be made of **Sâo Paolo** goalkeeper **Rogério Ceni** who scored **131** goals in his career.

COOL QUOTES

'In my teams, the striker is the first defender and the goalie is the first attacker.'

– Johan Cruyff

A FUNNY THING HAPPENED ...

During the 1930 World Cup semi-final between Argentina and the United States, the American trainer ran like a madman onto the pitch so he could shout at the referee. Unfortunately, as he threw his medical bag to the ground, it smashed a bottle of strong sleeping medicine, called chloroform, and the escaping gas knocked him out.

GEORGE BEST

George Best was Pelé's **FAVOURITE PLAYER OF ALL TIME**, which is a good enough reason to have him in here.

Originally from Northern Ireland, he was scouted when he was sixteen to play for Manchester United but came home after a few days because he was homesick. And that might have been the last we saw of one of the **TOP THREE PLAYERS IN FOOTBALLING LEGEND** except that after a chat with him and his parents, they decided to give him a second chance and the rest is football history. Hooray!

Best combined perfect **BALANCE**, great **STRENGTH** on the ball and deadly **FINISHING** to make him, for a while, the best player the world had ever seen. He wasn't big or aggressive but somehow he managed to ride out tackles from the toughest defenders who all looked like they were trying the break his ankles — mainly out of sheer frustration. Then he'd go on to score with that cheeky grin of his. But the greatest thing was to watch him change direction like a cat, slalom around backs and score from an impossible angle.

His greatest attribute — in an age where television was now in everyone's home — was that Georgie Best looked much, much COOLER than anyone else who had played football, now or then.

But this was where the trouble may have begun because pretty soon Best was as famous as any rock star and as popular as any Hollywood A Lister. Before long, he began to enjoy partying and being famous more than playing for Man U.

And the magic went away.

But, for a brief while he was David Beckham but with better skills, Pelé but hip, the Beatles but probably more fun to hang out with.

Going out too much and spending all his money may have cut short his time as a player but, as he said,

"They'll forget all the rubbish when I've gone and they'll remember the football. If only one person thinks I'm the best player in the world, that's good enough for me."

God bless you Georgie.

COMPETITIONS ...
AND PAST WINNERS

FIFA MEN'S WORLD CUP

Date/Location	Winners	Runners up	Score
1930 in Uruguay	Uruguay	Argentina	4-2
1934 in Italy	Italy	Czechoslovakia	2-1 (AET)
1938 in France	Italy	Hungary	4-2
1942 -	Not held		
1946 -	Not held		
1950 in Brazil	Uruguay	Brazil	2-1
1954 in Switzerland	West Germany	Hungary	3-2
1958 in Sweden	Brazil	Sweden	5-2
1962 in Chile	Brazil	Czechoslovakia	3-1
1966 in England	England	West Germany	4-2 (AET)
1970 in Mexico	Brazil	Italy	4-1
1974 in West Germany	West Germany	Netherlands	2-1
1978 in Argentina	Argentina	Netherlands	3-1 (AET)
1982 in Spain	Italy	West Germany	3-1
1986 in Mexico	Argentina	West Germany	3-2
1990 in Italy	West Germany	Argentina	1-0
1994 in United States	Brazil	Italy	0-0 (3-2 PKS)
1998 in France	France	Brazil	3-0
2002 in Japan/S. Korea	Brazil	Germany	2-0
2006 in Germany	Italy	France	1-1 (5-3 PKS)
2010 in South Africa	Spain	Netherlands	1-0 (AET)
2014 in Brazil	Germany	Argentina	1-0 (AET)
2018 in Russia	France	Croatia	4-2
2022 in Qatar	Will play in 2022		

AET = Added extra time

PKS = Penalty kicks

FIFA WOMEN'S WORLD CUP

Winning Years	Location	Winners	Runner-up	Results
1991	China	United States	Norway	2-1
1995	Sweden	Norway	Germany	2-0
1999	USA	United States	China	0-0 AET (5-4 Penalty)
2003	USA	Germany	Sweden	2-1
2007	China	Germany	Brazil	2-0
2011	Germany	Japan	United States	2-2 AET (3-1 aft)
2015	Canada	United States	Japan	5-2
2019	France	United States	Netherlands	2-0

FAMOUS CUPS AND LEAGUES AROUND THE WORLD

PREMIER LEAGUE WINNERS

Date	Winner	Runner-up
1992-93	Manchester United	Aston Villa
1993-94	Manchester United	Blackburn Rovers
1994-95	Blackburn Rovers	Manchester United
1995-96	Manchester United	Newcastle United
1996-97	Manchester United	Newcastle United
1997-98	Arsenal	Manchester United
1998-99	Manchester United	Arsenal
1999-2000	Manchester United	Arsenal
2000-01	Manchester United	Arsenal
2001-02	Arsenal	Liverpool
2002-03	Manchester United	Arsenal
2003-04	Arsenal	Chelsea
2004-05	Chelsea	Arsenal

2005-06	Chelsea	Manchester United
2006-07	Manchester United	Chelsea
2007-08	Manchester United	Chelsea
2008-09	Manchester United	Liverpool
2009-10	Chelsea	Manchester United
2010-11	Manchester United	Chelsea
2011-12	Manchester City	Manchester United
2012-13	Manchester United	Manchester City
2013-14	Manchester City	Liverpool
2014-15	Chelsea	Manchester City
2015-16	Leicester City	Arsenal
2016-17	Chelsea	Tottenham Hotspur
2017-18	Manchester City	Manchester United
2018-19	Manchester City	Liverpool
2019-20	Liverpool	Manchester City
2020-21	Manchester City	Manchester United
2021-22	Manchester City	Liverpool

FASCINATING FACT

Welsh forward Ian Rush is the most deadly striker in Liverpool Football Club history, scoring an astonishing 346 goals in 660 appearances. He also holds the club's record for the most goals in a single season, 50 scored in the 1983/84 season.

AFRICAN CUP OF NATIONS

Date	Location	Winner	Runner-up
2021	Cameroon	Senegal	Egypt
2019	Egypt	Algeria	Senegal
2017	Gabon	Cameroon	Egypt
2015	Equatorial Guinea	Ivory Coast	Ghana (pen)
2013	South Africa	Nigeria	Burkina Faso
2012	Gabon	Zambia	Ivory Coast (pen)
2010	Angola	Egypt	Ghana
2008	Ghana	Egypt	Cameroon

COPA LIBERTADORES

Date	Location	Winner	Runner-up
2021	Uruguay	Palmeiras	Flamengo
2020	Brazil	Palmeiras	Santos
2019	Brazil	Flamengo	River Plate
2018	Argentina	River Plate	Boca Juniors
2017	Brazil	Grêmio	Lanús N/A
2016	Columbia	Atlético Nacional	Independiente
2015	Argentina	River Plate	Tigres UANL

UEFA CHAMPIONS LEAGUE

Date	Location	Winner	Runner-up
2021-22	France	Real Madrid	Liverpool
2020-21	Portugal	Chelsea	Manchester City
2019-20	Portugal	Bayern Munich	Paris St-Germain
2018-19	Spain	Liverpool	Tottenham
2017-18	Ukraine	Real Madrid	Liverpool
2016-17	Cardiff	Real Madrid	Juventus
2015-16	Italy	Real Madrid	Atlético Madrid
2014-15	Germany	Barcelona	Juventus

UEFA EUROPA LEAGUE

Date	Location	Winner	Runner-up
2020-21	Poland	Villarreal	Man Utd
2019-20	Germany	Sevilla FC	Inter Milan
2018-19	Azerbaijan	Chelsea	Arsenal
2017-18	France	Athletico Madrid	Marseille
2016-17	Sweden	Man Utd	Ajax
2015-16	Switzerland	Sevilla FC	Liverpool
2014-15	Poland	Sevilla FC	Dnipro

UEFA EURO

Date	Location	Winner	Runner-up
2021	England	Italy	England
2016	France	Portugal	France
2012	Poland & Ukraine	Spain	Italy
2008	Austria & Switerland	Spain	Germany
2004	Portugal	Greece	Portugal
2000	Belgium & Netherlands	France	Italy
1996	England	Germany	Czech Republic
1992	Sweden	Denmark	Germany

COPA AMERICA

Date	Location	Winner	Runner-up
2011	Argentina	Uruguay	Paraguay
2015	Chile	Chile	Argentina
2016	USA	Chile	Argentina
2019	Rio	Brazil	Peru
2021	Rio	Argentina	Brazil

SAFF CHAMPIONSHIP

Date	Location	Winner	Runner-up
2009	Bangladesh	India	Maldives
2011	India	India	Afghanistan
2013	Nepal	Afghanistan	India
2015	India	India	Afghanistan
2018	Bangladesh	Maldives	India
2021	Maldives	India	Nepal

AFC ASIAN CUP

Date	Location	Winner	Runner-up
2019	UAE	Qatar	Japan
2015	Australia	Australia	South Korea
2011	Qatar	Japan	Austalia
2007	Indonesia	Iraq	Saudi Arabia

FIFA CONFEDERATIONS CUP

Date	Location	Winner	Runner-up
2005	France	France	Cameroon
2005	Germany	Brazil	Argentina
2009	South Africa	Brazil	United States
2013	Brazil	Brazil	Spain
2017	Russia	Germany	Chile

OLYMPIC GAMES

Men's	Host	Gold	Silver	Bronze
1996	USA	Nigeria	Argentina	Brazil
2000	Australia	Cameroon	Spain	Chile
2004	Greece	Argentina	Paraguay	Italy
2008	China	Argentina	Nigeria	Brazil
2012	UK	Mexico	Brazil	South Korea
2016	Brazil	Brazil	Germany	Nigeria
2020	Japan	Brazil	Spain	Mexico

Women's	Host	Gold	Silver	Bronze
1996	USA	USA	China	Norway
2000	Australia	Norway	USA	Germany
2004	Greece	USA	Brazil	Germany
2008	China	USA	Brazil	Germany
2012	UK	USA	Japan	Canada
2016	Brazil	Germany	Sweden	Canada
2020	Japan	Canada	Sweden	USA

FASCINATING FACT

The **Isles of Scilly Football League** is the **smallest** in the world with just **two teams** (**Woolpack Wanderers** and the **Garrison Gunners**) that play each other **eighteen times**. It is associated with the **FA**.

SPOTLIGHT ON PLAYERS

RASHFORD

Considered one of the **MOST VALUABLE** players in Europe, this Man U and England player has achieved an incredible amount in just a few years of playing – over 100 first class goals, 12 of which for England. A **GREAT ATHLETE**, he is also one of the most highly-regarded strikers currently playing anywhere, especially by other players who often have to double up just to tackle him.

And he's only going to get better.

He prefers the left wing, so he can use his better right foot and has inherited Wayne Rooney's prestigious Number 10 shirt.

BUT THAT IS NOT THE ONLY REASON FOR INCLUDING HIM IN SPOTLIGHT. RASHFORD IS UNDENIABLY ONE OF FOOTBALL'S GOOD GUYS – BOTH ON AND, ESPECIALLY, OFF THE PITCH.

His work campaigning for the homeless, against racism and child hunger showed everyone – even non-football fans – how a young football player from a humble background can MAKE THE WORLD A BETTER PLACE. His work on Child Food poverty got him a deserved MBE (Member of the British Empire).

And he is a highly successful author – his first book, *You are a Champion* is a massive best seller, leading him to work with publishers to increase reading for kids up and down the country.

Not bad for a 24 year old!

After Euro 2022, when a street mural of him was vandalised, the locals all came out and covered the rude and really rather shameful graffiti in messages of love and support.

He deserves all the praise he gets and more.

KEYWORDS
& WHAT THEY MEAN

Twelfth man

There are two different meanings. It either means fans who make so much noise that they help their team to win. It also may refer to a player who's not usually part of the starting eleven, but comes off the bench at some point during most of the matches.

Anti-football

When a side is being too defensive, shutting the game down. Dull.

Assist
When a great pass leads to a goal being scored.

Back of the net
A way to describe the ball crossing the goal line and smashing into the net.

Back-pass rule
Started to speed up play. A goalkeeper cannot pick up a ball if it has been passed back to him or her on purpose by another team member. They must kick it.

Ball-to-hand
When the contact between the hand and the ball is by mistake, therefore it shouldn't deserve a penalty. Often decided by whether the arm is in an 'unnatural position'. Complicated.

Bicycle kick
When a player jumps up, throws both feet in the air and kicks the ball in a pedalling motion to send the ball in the opposite direction they're facing. Also known as the overhead kick.

Boot it
Something yelled out by your teammates for you to kick the ball with full power to get it away.

Box-to-box player
A player who can easily play both sides: defensive and attacking. Like Yaya Touré or Patrick Vieira.

Brace
A word to describing a player who scores two goals in one game. 'Scoring a brace' is how to use it in a sentence.

Chip shot
A shot that is kicked from right underneath the ball to make it go over the opponent. See Lionel Messi almost any day of the week.

Class act
A player or even a manager who has an excellent attitude and manners off the field.

Clean sheet
When a team or goalkeeper plays without letting in a goal.

Cleats

The plastic or metallic bumps on the sole of football shoes that stop you falling over or sliding all the way across the pitch and into the car park.

Clinical finish

A shot that is taken very coolly and goes in the goal. The scorer of this goal is called the clinical finisher. Nothing to do with being a doctor.

Cracker

A breathtaking goal, mainly kicked from a long distance.

Cupset

When a smaller team beats a big team unexpectedly ('upset'+ 'cup').

'D'

The semi-circle at the edge of the penalty area, used to show the 10-yard distance around the penalty spot that lies outside the penalty area. Sometimes called the 'penalty arc'.

Dive

When a player tries to trick the referee by falling

over and rolling about like an idiot in order to win their team a penalty. Punishable by throwing in jail – no, not really – punishable by a warning, a yellow card or a match suspension.

Dr Griffin
Dr Griffin was the name of the invisible man in H.G. Wells' science fiction novel of the same name. So a pass 'to Dr Griffin' means a pass into an empty space that misses all your teammates.

Dummy run
An off-the-ball run made by an attacking player to create space for his or her teammate who has the ball. Used to trick the other side.

Equaliser
When a team scores a goal to draw level with the team they are playing against.

FC
Short for 'Football Club'. Simples.

Flip flap
Dribbling the ball in one direction after faking the dribble in the other direction with a sneaky body movement. Also known as the Snakebite because it

can look like the way a snake moves.

Fifty-fifty
When a tackle could be won by one of two players, each with an equal chance of getting the ball. Exciting.

First-time ball
Passing the ball to a teammate with a single touch.

Fixture
A match that hasn't been played yet.

Flick-on
A move where the attacking player hits a moving ball with their foot or head when it's passing by them without controlling it first. Bit like a first-time ball, but not quite.

Fortress
A home ground that very rarely loses a match.

Fox in a box
Someone who hangs about the goal, hoping to score easily.

Game of two halves
When a match has had two halves that are very

different (usually by the number of goals scored).

Ghost goal

When a goal isn't given, even when it crosses the goal line.

Group of death

A group in a tournament with really hard to beat teams.

Hairdryer treatment

When a manager shouts loudly at you in the changing room. Invented by former Manchester United manager, Alex Ferguson.

Hat trick

Scoring three goals in a match. It is called that after a businessman in Canada offered a free hat to anyone who scored three times in hockey. A Perfect Hat Trick is when a player scores three goals in a single match, one with the left foot, one with the right foot and one with a header.

Hoof

Kicking the ball towards the opposite goal as hard as you can.

Hospital pass
A pass that causes two players to crash into each other.

Howler
A terrible mistake by a player.

Hug the line
The instruction given to wing players to stay closer to the sidelines, especially when dribbling forward.

In his/her pocket
Refers to one player having completely bossed an opposition player during a match.

'It's coming home!'
Chorus from the 1990s hit 'Three Lions' by The Lightning Seeds, Frank Skinner and David Baddiel. The English have to sing or hum it, by law, every ten or fifteen minutes, each time England gets past the Group stages in an international competition.

Knuckleball
Kicking the ball (usually long range) so it hardly spins, which makes it weave about in a strange way and (hopefully) confuse the keeper.

Kop

Name for the stands right behind the goal: though generally used to refer to the stand at Liverpool's Anfield ground. At Man U it's called the Stretford end, for example. They say you're not a true Man U fan unless someone has peed in your pocket at the Stretford End. This refers to when it was all standing and you were squashed in like sardines, so people used to just wee where they were stood.

Lay-off pass

A short pass, usually sideways, kicked carefully into the space immediately in front of a teammate who is arriving at speed from behind the player making the pass. The player receiving the pass will then be able to take control of the ball without breaking stride, or (if they are close enough to the goal) attempt to score with a first-time shot.

Line-o

One of the nicknames for the assistant referees that work on the sidelines.

Lost the dressing room

A phrase to describe a situation in which the manager has lost control over and the respect of the players.

Magic sponge
Sponge with seemingly magical properties for healing injured players.

'Man on!'
The loud cry, as if you're up a mast on a sailing ship, to let a teammate with the ball know that an opponent is approaching or dangerously close by.

Mazy run
Another way of saying dribbling.

Midfield anchor
A very good defensive midfielder with the main mission of staying close to the defensive line and stopping attacks before they get going. See: Michael Essien or N'Golo Kanté.

Minnows
A small team.

Nutmeg
Kicking or putting the ball through an opponent's legs. Brilliant when it comes off.

Obstruction

Illegal defensive technique, when a defensive player who does not have control of the ball puts their body between the ball and an attacking opponent and blocks in order to prevent that opponent from reaching the ball.

Off the line

When someone (a hero) manages to just save the ball from crossing the goal line.

Panenka

A skill move used when taking a penalty kick. The player who is taking the penalty skilfully chips the ball over a diving goalkeeper, rather than kicking the ball as hard as they can.

Park the bus

Playing ultra-defensively so as not to let in any goals. A tactic mainly used by a team who are ahead in goals.

Play on (advantage)

When the referee does not blow their whistle (and everybody thinks they might) but there has not been a foul.

Pea roller

A slightly rubbish shot at goal that is so weak, there was never any way it was going to go in.

Poacher

See Fox in a box

Put in a shift

The situation where a player does everything right but fails to influence the game.

Row Z

The row in the stands that's the farthest from the pitch. Spectators usually mention it when a shot on goal is so hard but inaccurate it goes miles off target (into Row Z).

Run it off

If you get injured, someone is likely to say 'run it off' to you. What they really mean is they don't think it's that serious and if you get up and run about, you'll forget all about it. Annoyingly, they are often right. But don't try this if there is blood everywhere and your leg looks like it has an extra bend in it or could be starring in a zombie movie.

Screamer

Huge kick, from a long way off that gets the crowd on their feet, shouting their collective heads off.

Seal dribble

Running past a defender, whilst bouncing the ball on your head. Like a seal.

Showboat

Showing off for fans after scoring easily. Poor form.

Silverware

Another word for trophies.

Sitter

A shocking miss by an attacker that was considered to be immensely easy to score from.

Squeaky-bum time

The end of a match that is very close between two teams (and exciting/terrifying).

Switch

Moving the ball from one edge of the pitch to the other quickly, mostly by a long pass ball.

Target man

A forward who is often targeted by crosses, long balls, and high passes for their aerial superiority (usually because they are tall, with a head like an anvil) and ability as a finisher. See: Zlatan Ibrahimović, Peter Crouch, Didier Drogba, amongst others.

Toe punt

Kicking the ball (hard) with the end of the toe.

Treble

Winning three major competitions in a single season.

Video Assistant Referee (VAR)

Only used to correct 'clear and obvious' errors including: goals, penalties, red cards and mistaken identity. The final decision is always taken by the on-field referee.

(Hit the) woodwork

Having the ball strike one of the posts or crossbar of the goal.

OTHER TITLES IN THE STUPENDOUS SPORTS SERIES OUT NOW:

RAMPAGING RUGBY

First in the comedy series **Stupendous Sports** which aims to do for **PE** what Horrible Histories did for **Year 7 History**.

OTHER TITLES IN THE STUPENDOUS SPORTS SERIES OUT SHORTLY:

CRACKING CRICKET

Each chapter will have **cartoons**, **player tips** your coach won't tell you, **explanations**, fascinating **facts** and – yes – **funny stories**. It will hopefully teach you just as much about the **spirit** of the game as the **rules**.

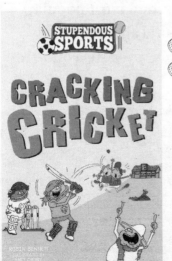

Out in time for the

- ⚪ **ICC World Cup 2023**
- ⚪ **'Training Shorts'** on YouTube and **www.stupendoussports.com**

DID YOU KNOW?

Cricket is thought to have started as a way for **English shepherds** to pass the time whilst looking after **sheep**, who were the first **fielders** and probably no worse at it than your little brother.

It started in **16th Century** in **England**, a game in **Aleppo** in **Syria** was written about in **1676**! And the first ever **international** was played between the **US** and **Canada** in **New York** in **1844**.

Test cricket is one of the **longest** games in the world (normally **5 days**). The longest match ever was between **England** and **South Africa** – it went on for **2 weeks**!

It is estimated that there are nearly **60 million players** of cricket in the world with over **2 billion fans,** which makes it the **second most popular** sport in the world after football. It is played in over **100 countries**.

WWW.STUPENDOUSSPORTS.COM

THE PLACE FOR KIDS WHO ARE MAD ON SPORT!

- SPORTS NEWS FOR KIDS
- BOOK AUTHOR VISITS
- CARTOONS
- FUNNY STORIES
- AUDIO DOWNLOADS AND VIDEOS
- NEWS ON FORTHCOMING EVENTS

STUPENDOUS SPORTS FANCLUB!

Look out for special offers on signed books, sports kit, merchandise (toys, stickers, pens – you name it!) and tickets to sporting events!

ACKNOWLEDGMENTS

No book is ever one hundred per cent down to one person – as with all the best things in life (including football), it's a team effort. I wouldn't have been able to give you a book about football nearly half as good without the amazing Matt Cherry and his even more amazing illustrations. I am also incalculably grateful to John-Mark Hanrahan, Chris Bennett, Penny Thomas, Leonie Lock, Rebecca Lloyd and everyone at Firefly Press for correcting my spelling, checking my facts and laughing in all the right places.

… and a quick note on those facts: whilst we have taken care to check rules, stats and facts, football is a fluid game: rules change, facts can be disputed and records are broken all the time. If anything is wrong or has changed since the book was written, the fault is mine. This is a book about the spirit football more than anything and – much like the beautiful game itself – it may have it flaws and faults but its heart is in the right place, I hope.

ROBIN BENNETT
MATT CHERRY

STUPENDOUS SPORTS

CHECK OUT THE FIRST
CHAPTER OF

RAMPAGING
RUGBY

CHAPTER 1:HISTORY

Who on Earth invented rugby?

Including why rugby balls look like rubbish footballs and how they killed Mrs Lindon.

Like most sports that involve:

- two **teams** that **hate** each other
- a (sort of) **round object**
- lots of **pushing** and **shoving**

rugby almost certainly started a very long time ago indeed – most likely when one group of barbarians chopped the head off someone (let's call him Bol) who lived in the village next door. Being barbarians (and it's no surprise to anyone that there is actually a team called the **Barbarians** today), they then started throwing poor Bol's head around for their own amusement, at which point everyone

in Bol's village ran around to put an immediate stop to all that fun at their expense. This may well have been the origin of the phrase '**can we have our Bol back?**'

The fight that followed usually went on for days, the head being '**passed**' **backwards** to make sure the other '**team**' couldn't get their grubby paws on it.

Eventually, both sides ended up in the village pond at which point they all realised:

- what a great time they'd had **knocking** each other's **teeth** out
- that chilling in a warm muddy **pond** with your mates is **ace**
- that no one had especially **liked** Bol in the first place.

Letting off a bit of steam in this highly entertaining, before-the-internet way was repeated in literally thousands of villages all over the place until chopping your neighbour's head off became unfashionable and everyone started playing football anyway.

Scroll forward a few centuries and we find ourselves at **Rugby School**, on the outskirts of the town of Rugby, in England. At a game of *football*.

It is the year **1823**.

Nothing about that day or the game must have seemed unusual, unless your name happened to be **William Webb Ellis**. Master Webb Ellis was a pupil at the school and no one knows much about him except that he decided to pick up the ball up and run with it.

Basically, he **cheated**.

However, instead of being punished by being hung by his **underpants** from the nearest crossbar, everyone on the pitch thought *now why didn't I think of that?* and pretty soon they were all at it.

> **NOTE** *There are some people who do not believe this happened at all, but everyone agrees that this version of rugby (ie one that doesn't involve a severed head) was first played at Rugby School and then introduced by ex-pupils to the rest of the world, where it caught on pretty quickly.*

By 1845 rugby had its own set of rules and ... *[drum roll]* ... **funny balls** *[cymbal clash]*!

FASCINATING FACT There's a rumour going around that **basketball** was invented to keep rugby players fit **off season**.

'Rugby is not a contact sport, it's a collision sport'

– Anonymous

Rebel girls

Women's rugby started a long time ago too.

The earliest known player is **Emily Valentine**.

In **1887**, at the tender age of **10**, she was watching her brothers play rugby and the call came for an **extra player**. Even though the idea of a girl playing rugby was about as strange as an octopus singing light opera, she got stuck in.

In **1991** the first **Women's Rugby World Cup** was organised by four determined English women, **Deborah Griffin**, **Sue Dorrington**, **Alice Cooper** and **Mary Forsyth**, and held in and around **Cardiff**, South Wales. Despite having little money and even less official support, 12 teams turned up from as far afield as the **USSR**, **Canada**, **Japan** and **New Zealand**.

The

USA beat **England** in the final.

In a lot of **Asian** and **South American** countries the numbers of girls and boys playing rugby are pretty evenly split – **50/50**.

So, we're going to need more bullet points...

- **Forty per cent** of rugby's 800 million-strong fanbase is **female**.
- More girls have **started playing** rugby than boys
  in the past two years.
- The number of registered female players has risen to **2.7 million**, up from just **45,000** in 1995.
- Double Grand Slam winners **England** became the first fully **professional** women's team in January **2019**.

'We firmly believe that the development of **women in rugby** is the single **greatest opportunity** for our sport to grow in the next decade,' said World Rugby chairman **Sir Bill Beaumont**.

FASCINATING FACT Barette was a popular full-contact sport adapted from rugby union in the 1920s and played by women.

Tackles were only allowed around the waist, teams were 12-a-side, and playing time and pitch dimensions were slightly smaller.

The ball

I think we can all agree that one of the most exciting aspects of rugby today is the fact that a rugby ball, passed by someone who knows what they are doing, resembles a **dangerous missile**. However, when the ball bounces, it behaves in a way that succeeds in making professional sportspeople look like **complete clowns**.

So, it can fly as smoothly as a rocket or jump around like someone with a small army of **bullet ants** down their shorts. This means that rugby is never predictable. Anything can happen and anything often does. This is **great**.

FASCINATING FACT During World War II, the Germans banned rugby as it was a bit too British and reminded them the British hadn't surrendered yet.

However, nobody thought about this 200 years ago – they just knew they wanted balls that were a bit **different** from footballs (mainly bigger) – and so they went to a couple of local shoemakers called **Richard Lindon** and **Bernardo Solano** and asked them to have a go at making one, since they were obviously good at stitching things together.

Nowadays, we have lots of things that inflate (mainly made of rubber, plastic or bubblegum). In those days, all they had that could be blown up and stay blown up for 90 minutes or more were **bladders** (the thing that keeps your pee from sloshing around in your tummy is also very good at keeping air in).

Obviously they couldn't use **human** bladders, so they used the next best thing: **pigs' bladders**.

But bladders aren't round – ask any doctor (or shoemaker) – which meant they came out shaped like a **cucumber who has spent a lot of time in the gym**.

Also, some of the pigs' bladders weren't exactly fresh, and **Mr Lindon's wife**, whose job it was to blow the balls up, contracted a nasty disease from rotten bladders which unfortunately **killed** her.

At this point, Richard Lindon sensibly decided to start using **rubber** instead.